BY JENNA TOLLI

TAYLOR SWIFT

from the Beginning

EVERYTHING TAYLOR SWIFT

(Gareth's Version)

Gareth Stevens
PUBLISHING

Please visit our website, www.garethstevens.com. For a free color catalog of all our high-quality books, call toll free 1-800-542-2595 or fax 1-877-542-2596.

Library of Congress Cataloging-in-Publication Data

Names: Tolli, Jenna, author.
Title: Taylor Swift from the beginning / Jenna Tolli.
Description: Buffalo, New York : Gareth Stevens Publishing, 2025. | Series: Everything Taylor Swift (Gareth's version) | Includes index.
Identifiers: LCCN 2024031169 | ISBN 9781482469424 (library binding) | ISBN 9781482469417 (paperback) | ISBN 9781482469431 (ebook)
Subjects: LCSH: Swift, Taylor, 1989—Juvenile literature. | Singers–United States–Biography–Juvenile literature. | Country musicians–United States–Biography–Juvenile literature.
Classification: LCC ML3930.S989 T66 2025 | DDC 782.42164092 [B]–dc23/eng/20240705
LC record available at https://lccn.loc.gov/2024031169

Published in 2025 by
Gareth Stevens Publishing
2544 Clinton Street
Buffalo, NY 14224

Designer: Tanya Dellaccio Keeney
Editor: Kristen Nelson

Photo credits: Cover (friendship bracelet) Yuliqwiart/Shutterstock.com; cover (Taylor) Everett Collection/Shutterstock.com; cover (background) Anastasiia Smiian/Shutterstock.com; p. 5 mpi67/MediaPunch/IPx/AP Images; p. 7 Ritu Manoj Jethani/Shutterstock.com; p. 9 Christian Bertrand/Shutterstock.com; p. 10 Foxys Graphic/Shuttertock.com; p. 11 Chris Pizzello/Invision/AP Images; p. 13 (top) 4kclips/Shutterstock.com; p. 13 (bottom) Joseph Hendrickson/Shutterstock.com; p. 15 AP Images; p. 17 Carla Sloke/Shuttertock.com; p. 19 A.PAES/Shutterstock.com; p. 21 Courtesy of Brian Cantoni/Flickr.com; p. 23 AFF/Alamy Images; p. 24 s_bukley/Shuttertock.com; p. 25 Catrina Haze/Shutterstock.com; p. 27 Christian Bertrand/Shuttertock.com.

Printed in the United States of America

CPSIA compliance information: Batch #CWGS25: For further information contact Gareth Stevens at 1-800-542-2595.

CONTENTS

BOLDFACE WORDS APPEAR IN GLOSSARY

THE BEGINNING

Taylor Alison Swift was born on December 13, 1989. She was born in Reading, Pennsylvania, and grew up in a town nearby called Wyomissing.

Her parents' names are Scott and Andrea. Her father worked in **finance** and her mother worked in **marketing**. Her younger brother, Austin, was born in 1992. When Taylor and Austin were born, their mom stayed home to raise them. The Swift family lived on a Christmas tree farm when Taylor was growing up.

KNOW IT ALL

Taylor wrote a song called "Christmas Tree Farm" about where she grew up. You can see old clips of her and her family living there in the song's music video.

Taylor is still very close with her family today! She often travels with her mom, Andrea, on tour.

GROWING UP

Taylor had a lot of interests when she was a kid. Growing up, she rode horses. She even took part in horseback riding competitions, or contests. She also took acting classes in New York City and went to some **auditions** there too.

Taylor liked reading and writing. She read **poetry** and wrote her own poems. Taylor even wrote a whole book when she was young! She would often write in journals about her life and goals.

KNOW IT ALL

When Taylor was in fourth grade, she won a national poetry contest!

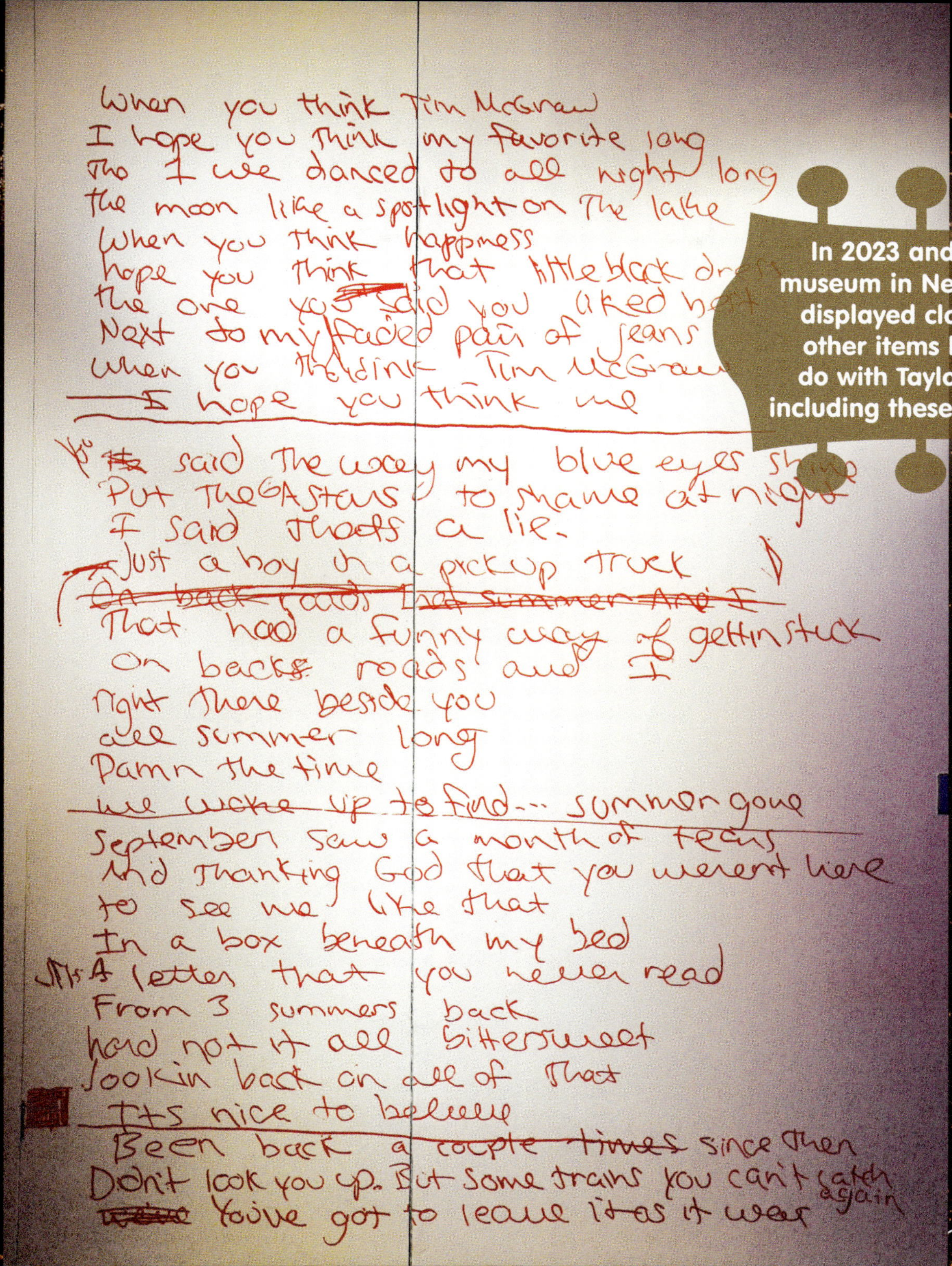
When you think Tim McGraw
I hope you think my favorite song
The 1 we danced to all night long
The moon like a spotlight on the lake
When you think happiness
hope you think that little black dress
the one you said you liked best
Next to my faded pair of jeans
When you think Tim McGraw
I hope you think me
You said the way my blue eyes shine
Put the Georgia stars to shame at night
I said that's a lie.
Just a boy in a pickup truck
On back roads that summer And I
That had a funny way of gettin stuck
on back roads and I
right there beside you
all summer long
Damn the time
we woke up to find... summer gone
September saw a month of tears
And thanking God that you weren't here
to see me like that
In a box beneath my bed
A letter that you never read
From 3 summers back
hard not it all bittersweet
lookin back on all of that
Its nice to believe
Been back a couple times since then
Don't look you up. But some trains you can't catch again
You've got to leave it as it was

In 2023 and 2024, a museum in New York City displayed clothes and other items having to do with Taylor's music, including these song lyrics!

EARLY INTEREST IN MUSIC

Taylor always loved music and has been singing since she was very young. She started taking singing lessons as a child.

She has also been **performing** since she was a kid, including singing at sporting events in Pennsylvania. She was **excited** to sing in front of a lot of people. One of her earliest performances was singing "The Star-Spangled Banner" at a Philadelphia 76ers basketball game in April 2002. She performed the song in front of more than 20,000 people that day!

IN TAYLOR'S WORDS

"I started singing in front of crowds when I was 10, and it was a little scary at first. Anything you've just started doing is going to be scary."
(*CMT.com*, November 12, 2007)

THE REPUTATION STADIUM TOUR
WEMBLEY STADIUM
LONDON, UNITED KINGDOM
JUNE 2018

Today, Taylor performs in sports **stadiums** for her own concerts!

INFLUENCES

Taylor enjoyed listening to female country artists like Shania Twain, Faith Hill, and The Chicks. They were some of her first **influences** for beginning a country music **career**.

Taylor found out that Shania Twain and Faith Hill started out in Nashville, Tennesee. Nashville has a lot of record labels and places for new country artists to play music. Taylor wanted to move there, but it was far from her home.

It would have taken Taylor's family more than 10 hours to drive to Nashville from their home in Pennsylvania.

SHANIA TWAIN

Female country artists like Shania Twain and Faith Hill had great success in the late 1990s and early 2000s. This is when Taylor started to work hard on singing.

MOVE TO TENNESSEE

Taylor visited Nashville when she was 11. She took CDs of her singing to record companies around the city. She didn't get a record deal. But Taylor kept going. She started writing her own music and learned to play the guitar! She started playing the guitar at age 12.

When Taylor was about 14, her family moved to Hendersonville, Tennessee, a town close to Nashville. This helped Taylor get to know more people in the music **industry**.

IN TAYLOR'S WORDS

"My family has always been really cool because they have said to me, 'We're 100 percent behind this dream, but if you have another dream tomorrow, we're 100 percent behind that too.'"
(*Teen Vogue*, November 25, 2008)

KNOW IT ALL

Taylor and her mom filmed part of their trip to drop off CDs in Nashville. In the **documentary** *Miss Americana*, which came out in 2020, you can see them talking about how it went.

The Country Music Hall of Fame and Museum in Nashville opened the Taylor Swift Education Center in 2013. Visitors can learn about music, songwriting, and Taylor's early career!

WRITING HER OWN MUSIC

By this time, Taylor wanted to be an artist that writes and sings her own songs. She began to work with Liz Rose, a country music songwriter. Taylor brought song ideas to Liz after school, and they worked on them together.

Taylor did sign a contract to start writing music as a young teenager, but it didn't come with a **guarantee** to create an album of her own songs. She looked for a label that would value her songwriting and help her put out an album.

IN TAYLOR'S WORDS

"I know that without me writing my own songs I wouldn't be here."
(*Miss Americana*, 2020)

Taylor and Liz Rose wrote songs that became hits! In 2010, they won a Grammy for the song "White Horse," which they co-wrote.

RECORD DEAL

Taylor continued to write songs and perform in Nashville. In November 2004, she sang and played guitar at the Bluebird Cafe, a well-known place in Nashville that has small concerts for songwriters.

Scott Borchetta, the founder of a new record label called Big Machine Records, went to see Taylor's performance. He wanted to work with her and later offered her a record deal. Borchetta signed Taylor to Big Machine when she was only a teenager!

Lots of people visit the Bluebird Cafe in Nashville to see musicians play. People from record labels also visit to find new music artists.

BEGINNING OF AN ERA

Taylor signed a contract with Big Machine Records to make six albums over 13 years with them. She wanted to work with people who would value her songwriting, and the team at Big Machine said they would do that.

Taylor continued working with Liz Rose and other songwriters she met through the record label. She wrote about her life and what she saw happening around her. She started to record songs and create her first album over the next year.

KNOW IT ALL

In 2018, Taylor's deal with Big Machine Recordsended. In recent years, Taylor has started rerecording the albums she made with Big Machine to own the **master recordings** of her music.

It was important to Taylor to find a record label where she could sing her original songs. She loved writing songs and wanted to share them.

FOCUS ON MUSIC

Taylor went to high school in Hendersonville for two years. After she got her record deal, and especially when her music started to get popular, she needed to finish high school without going into school every day.

She switched to a new school that did home schooling. Home schooling is a way of taking classes at home or somewhere other than in a school. This way, she could finish her education while she was building her music career.

KNOW-IT-ALL

Taylor's high school diploma came in the mail while she was on tour. A diploma is the piece of paper that says someone has finished their work at a school.

IN TAYLOR'S WORDS

"There's something really exciting about getting to live your dream and continue your education at the same time."
(*Associated Press*, July 2008)

Taylor earned good grades in school and finished up her high school work while on tour!

FIRST SINGLE

Taylor released her first single, or song, in June 2006. It was called "Tim McGraw." Taylor wrote it while she was still in high school!

Tim McGraw is a famous country singer, and Taylor was a big fan of his. The song is about loving someone who moved away, and hoping they would have good memories of the time spent with you. This song was very popular and helped start her path to becoming the superstar we know today!

TIM MCGRAW

FAITH HILL

In 2007, Taylor won an award, or prize, for the music video for "Tim McGraw."

KNOW IT ALL

Seven years after "Tim McGraw" came out, in 2013, Taylor recorded a song with Tim McGraw himself! The song is titled "Highway Don't Care."

FIRST ALBUM

Taylor's first album, *Taylor Swift*, came out in October 2006. She wrote some of the songs on the album with other songwriters and some all on her own. Taylor was just 16 years old when the album came out.

The album was a success! It reached number 1 on the *Billboard* Top Country Albums chart. It also got to number 5 on the *Billboard* 200 chart, which is a weekly list of the most popular albums from all types of music.

The album *Taylor Swift* has sold more than 5 million copies as of 2024!

SINGLES FROM *TAYLOR SWIFT*

"Tim McGraw"
"Teardrops on My Guitar"
"Our Song"
"Picture to Burn"
"Should've Said No"

FOLLOWING HER DREAM

After her first album, Taylor made 10 more and four rerecordings—so far! With her fourth album, she started to move away from just country music and make pop music, which she is most well-known for today.

Taylor has won more than 100 awards for her music, including 40 American Music Awards—more than any artist in history. Her story and music have made many young musicians want to follow their dreams, just like she did!

Taylor now performs in front of thousands of people at her concerts! The Eras Tour in 2023 and 2024 brought in over $1 billion dollars in ticket sales.

TAYLOR'S START

December 13, 1989	TAYLOR IS BORN IN PENNSYLVANIA.
April 2002	SHE SINGS AT A PHILADELPHIA 76ERS GAME.
2003-2004	SHE SIGNS HER FIRST MUSIC CONTRACT.
	THE SWIFT FAMILY MOVES TO THE NASHVILLE AREA.
November 2004	TAYLOR PERFORMS IN THE BLUEBIRD CAFE.
2005	SHE SIGNS A RECORD DEAL WITH BIG MACHINE RECORDS.
June 2006	TAYLOR'S FIRST SINGLE, "TIM MCGRAW," COMES OUT.
October 2006	*TAYLOR SWIFT* ALBUM COMES OUT.

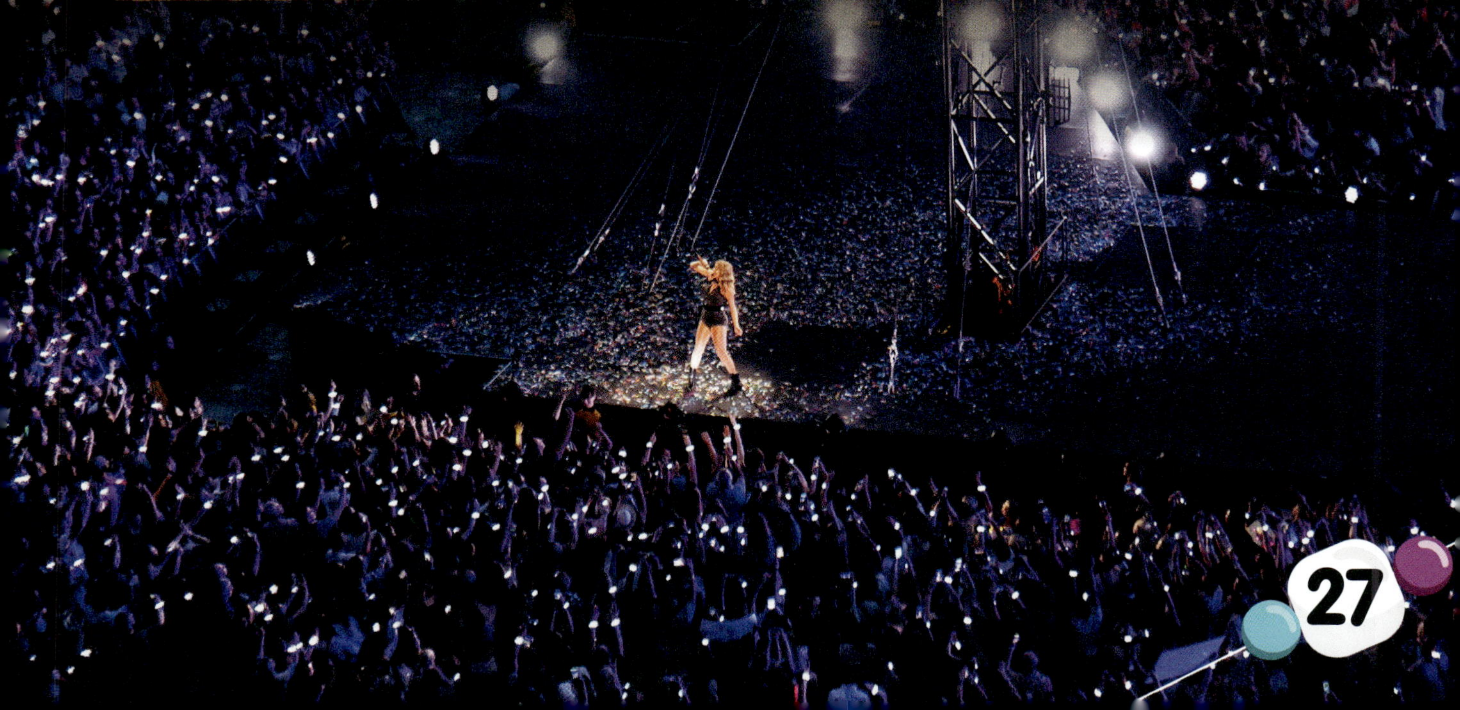

ACTIVITY: MAKE A DREAM BOARD

A dream is something you really want, deep in your heart. It might seem a little like a goal, but it's often bigger than that! This project helps you discover what your dreams are and helps you visualize them.

MATERIALS:

- poster board (any color)
- paper to draw on (any color)
- colored markers
- stickers
- glitter
- paint
- magazines (and permission to cut them up)
- scissors
- glue
- a computer, tablet, or phone that's connected to the internet (and permission to use it to look for quotes)

STEP 1

Think about your dreams. Write a list. Get creative and think about all different parts of your life including your friends, family, future career, and activities.

Examples: travel to Italy, become a pastry chef, get a part in the school play, start a band

STEP 2

Draw pictures of each dream you've listed. You may also look through magazines and find pictures that represent the dream. Cut out the pictures.

STEP 3

Use your internet-connected device to look up quotes that relate to your dream or that you find interesting. You might want to add some Taylor Swift lyrics! Write or print these out.

STEP 4

Use glue to attach your pictures and quotes to your dream board. Use stickers, glitter, paint, or other craft supplies too.

You may choose to hang your dream board in your room to remind you of your big dreams. Or you may want to share it with your friends or family!

GLOSSARY

audition: A try out.

career: The job someone chooses to do for a long time.

documentary: A movie presenting information about someone's life or other topic.

excited: Being very eager or energetic about something.

finance: Having to do with money.

guarantee: To promise that some condition holds or will be fulfilled.

industry: The businesses that provide a particular product or service.

influence: To have an effect on.

marketing: The job of making the public aware of services or items for sale.

master recording: The official, original recording of a song. It is sometimes just called a master.

perform: A public presentation or exhibition.

poetry: Poems, or pieces of writing in verse that sometimes tell a story.

stadium: A large building where a sports team plays.

FOR MORE INFORMATION

Books

Kawa, Katie. *Taylor Swift: Making a Difference as a Songwriter.* New York, NY: KidHaven Publishing, 2022.

Olson, Elsie. *Taylor Swift*. Minneapolis, MN: Checkerboard Library, 2022.

Websites

Taylor Swift
www.taylorswift.com/
Find more information about Taylor on her official website!

Universal Music Publishing Group: Taylor Swift
https://www.umusicpub.com/us/Artists/T/Taylor-Swift.aspx
See what is next for Taylor's music on her record label's website.

Publisher's note to educators and parents: Our editors have carefully reviewed these websites to ensure that they are suitable for students. Many websites change frequently, however, and we cannot guarantee that a site's future contents will continue to meet our high standards of quality and educational value. Be advised that students should be closely supervised whenever they access the internet.

INDEX